NO MORE DEAD DOGS

by
Gordon Korman

Teacher Guide

Written by
Sharan Farmer

Note

The Hyperion Paperbacks for Children edition of the book, ©2000 by Gordon Korman, was used to prepare this guide. Page references may differ in other editions. Novel ISBN: 0-7868-1601-5

Please note: Please assess the appropriateness of this book for the age level and maturity of your students prior to reading and discussing it with them.

ISBN-10: 1-58130-946-5
ISBN-13: 978-1-58130-946-1

To order, contact your local school supply store, or—

Copyright infringement is a violation of Federal

© 2006 by Novel Units, Inc., Bulverde, Texas. All rights reserved
be reproduced, translated, stored in a retrieval system, or transm
(electronic, mechanical, photocopying, recording, or otherwise)
from ECS Learning Systems, Inc.

Photocopying of student worksheets by a classroom teacher
purchased this publication for his/her own class is permissible. Reproduction of any part of this
publication for an entire school or for a school system, by for-profit institutions and tutoring centers,
or for commercial sale is strictly prohibited.

Novel Units is a registered trademark of ECS Learning Systems, Inc.
Printed in the United States of America.

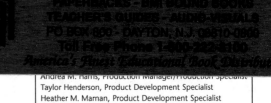

Andrea M. Harris, Production Manager/Production Specialist
Taylor Henderson, Product Development Specialist
Heather M. Marnan, Product Development Specialist
Suzanne K. Mammen, Curriculum Specialist
Pamela Rayfield, Product Development Specialist
Jill Reed, Product Development Specialist
Adrienne Speer, Production Specialist

Table of Contents

Skills and Strategies

Thinking
Research, compare/contrast, brainstorming, identifying attributes, analyzing details, drawing conclusions

Comprehension
Predicting, sequencing, main idea, inference, summarizing

Writing
List, journal, riddle, letter, newspaper story, research, memo, essay, playbill, song lyrics, review, haiku/acrostic poetry, play scenes, direct quotes

Listening/Speaking
Debate, discussion, monologue, interview

Vocabulary
Parts of speech, definitions, root words, synonyms/antonyms, word origins

Literary Elements
Stereotypes, point of view, figurative language, allusion, plot development, dialogue, epiphany, irony, author's style, slang, characterization, suspense, setting, sarcasm

Across the Curriculum
Social Studies—jury oaths, maps, Chinese water torture, George Washington; Art—magazine cover, scenery sketch, flier design, playbill design, comic strip, book jacket, diorama, poster; Drama—acting, facial expressions, role play, stage setting; Math—graphs, charts; Science—Indian summer; Music—songs; Library skills—dictionary, thesaurus, fiction book search

Genre: young-adult fiction

Setting: present-day, Bedford Middle School

Point of View: multiple first person

Conflict: person vs. person, person vs. self

Themes: friendship, values, honesty, talents, stereotypes

Tone: humorous

Date of First Publication: 2000

Summary

Eighth-grade football hero Wallace Wallace has been sentenced to detention for writing a bad review of *Old Shep, My Pal*, which just happens to be English teacher Mr. Fogelman's favorite novel. His detention takes him out of football practice and puts him right in the middle of the drama club, which is practicing for a production of…*Old Shep, My Pal* with Mr. Fogelman as the director! Wallace refuses to write a favorable review of the novel. He finds it boring because the dog dies in the end, as happens in so many other books about dogs. His detention will continue until he writes a favorable book report of the novel for Mr. Fogelman. The football team is irate that their star player is missing practice, and the team is losing every game. Drama club members are incensed that a football player has been thrown into their midst. And all this happens because Wallace truly believes that honesty is the best policy. But as Wallace begins making suggestions to improve the dated dialogue and stilted predictable action of the play, drama club members take on a renewed interest in the play, much to the chagrin of Mr. Fogelman and drama club president Rachel Turner. Then someone begins to sabotage the play. Likely suspects include Wallace and members of the football team. Despite the setbacks, the play transforms into a wild, rollicking production, and Wallace learns the true meaning of friendship. Told from multiple viewpoints, the novel is a lively story that explores the angst of middle-school students, the misconceptions of stereotypes, and the value of true friends.

Characters

Wallace Wallace—eighth-grade football hero sent to detention for being honest in his review of the novel *Old Shep, My Pal*

Rick Falconi—middle-school football quarterback; Wallace's friend who wants him back on the team

Mike "Feather" Wrigley—middle-school football player; coach's son

Steve Cavanaugh—middle-school football player; team captain; Wallace's ex-best friend

Rachel Turner—seventh-grade actress and president of the drama club who resents Wallace's presence at play practice

Trudi Davis—Rachel's best friend

Nathaniel Spitzner—whiny drama club member

Vito Brundia, Leticia Ogden, Leo Samuels, Everton Wu, Kelly Ramone—drama club members

Mr. Fogelman—young English teacher and play director whose favorite novel is *Old Shep, My Pal*

All rights reserved

Coach Wrigley—football coach; Feather's dad

Mrs. Wallace—Wallace Wallace's mom

Dr. Chechik—Bedford Middle School principal

Parker Schmidt—alias Porker Zit; reporter for the school newspaper who doesn't fact check

Rory Piper—Rollerblading dogcatcher in the play

Dylan Turner—Rachel's 10-year-old brother; Wallace's biggest fan

Dead Mangoes—teen rock band

Laszlo Tamas—16-year-old eighth grader from Hungary

About the Author

Gordon Korman was born October 23, 1963, in Montreal, Quebec, and moved with his family to the Toronto area in 1971. He wrote his first novel, *This Can't Be Happening at Macdonald Hall*, as a writing project when he was 12 years old. Two years later, he submitted his manuscript to Scholastic Canada, where it was published when he was 14 years old. At 16, he won the Air Canada award for the most promising young author in Canada. Korman has written over 50 novels for middle school students and young adults. His book series, *The Monday Night Football Club*, was the inspiration for the Disney TV series *The Jersey*.

Korman received his bachelor's degree from New York University in 1985, with a major in dramatic and visual writing and a minor in motion picture and television. He and his wife Michelle, a third-grade teacher, live on Long Island, New York, with their three children.

Gordon Korman's hallmark in children's literature is his humorous novels. He transforms real-life situations into hilarious plots with his vivid imagination. Some of his later works are suspense and action-adventure novels.

"I'd like to think kids really hear me," Korman said. "I'm not sure why that is, but...I suspect it's because I view childhood not as the waiting period until one can be a 'real' person, but as a here and now, that has to be lived with dignity and meaning." His characters are generally "movers and shakers"—kids who do something about the situation they are in—and his readers tend to like that.

Recent awards and accolades received by Korman include the 2003 Young Reader's Choice Award, Intermediate Division; Rebecca Caudill Young Readers' Book Award Nominee 2004; California Young Reader Medal Middle School/Junior High Level Nominee; and the Young Hoosier Book Award 2003–04 Nominee.

Other works by Korman include: *Son of Interflux* (1986), *The Zucchini Warriors* (1988), *Macdonald Hall Goes Hollywood* (1991), *Something Fishy at Macdonald Hall* (1995), *Liar, Liar, Pants On Fire* (1997), *The Sixth Grade Nickname Game* (1998), *Nose Pickers from Outer Space* (1999), *Island trilogy* (2001), *Son Of the Mob* (2002), *Everest trilogy* (2002), *Dive trilogy* (2003), and the *On the Run* series (2004–05).

All rights reserved

Initiating Activities

Use one or more of the following to introduce the novel.

1. Predictions: Have students read the dedication at the beginning of the novel and predict what they think "Rick-isms" might be.

2. Stereotypes: Have students discuss stereotypes by viewing movie clips from the animated film *Shrek*. Make a list of the stereotypes depicted in the film and describe each.

3. Stereotypes: Have students explore stereotypes by reviewing the cast of characters found at the beginning of the novel. Have them discuss the possible character traits of each type of character: football quarterback, drama club actress, mom, coach, teacher, rock star, etc.

4. Critical Thinking: Have students debate the expression: "Honesty is the best policy."

5. Predictions: Based on the title, the artwork on the front and back covers, the names of the characters in the character list, and the "disclaimer" found at the bottom of the character page, have students predict the type of novel this might be.

6. Predictions: Have students scan the novel and discuss the format of the book, which is not written in chapters. Discuss what the section entries might mean.

Vocabulary Activities

1. Parts of Speech: Have students keep a vocabulary journal while reading the novel by writing down all vocabulary words, their parts of speech, and their definitions as used in context.

2. Root Words: Have students make a T-chart of the vocabulary words and their roots, if applicable.

3. Puzzles: Have students create a word search to trade with classmates.

4. Definitions: Have students create quizzes matching the vocabulary words with their definitions.

5. Vocabulary Bee: Divide students into teams to compete in a vocabulary bee.

6. Synonyms/Antonyms: Have students use a dictionary and/or thesaurus to find synonyms or antonyms for vocabulary words.

7. Word Origins: Using a dictionary, have students find the origins of vocabulary words.

8. Dictionary: Have students conduct dictionary drills by calling out a vocabulary word. The first person who finds the word reads the part of speech and definitions.

9. Riddles: Have students compose riddles about a vocabulary word, giving clues such as definition, part of speech, word origin, word relationships, etc. Classmates can then solve the riddles.

All rights reserved

Story Map

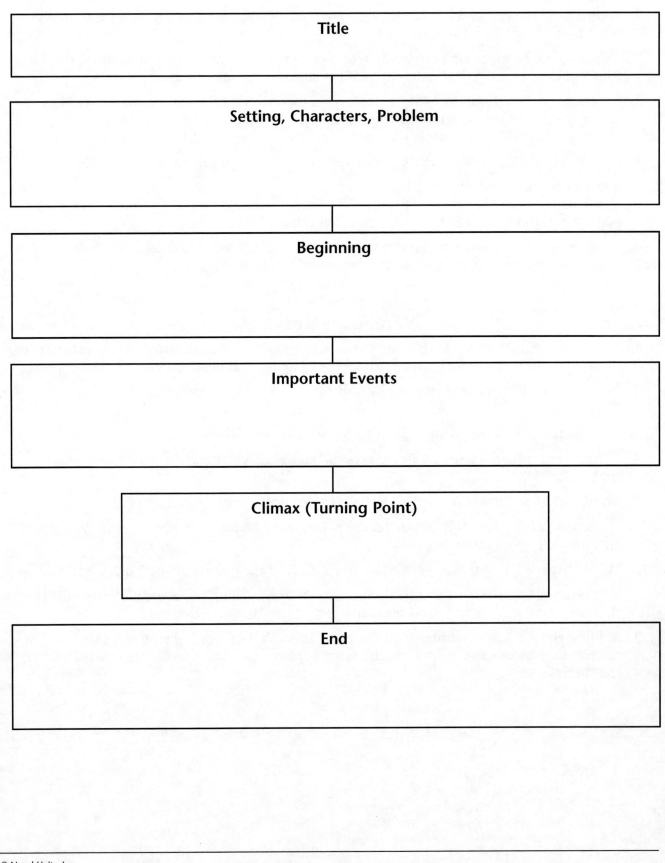

Title

Setting, Characters, Problem

Beginning

Important Events

Climax (Turning Point)

End

All rights reserved

 © Novel Units, Inc.

Using Predictions

We all make predictions as we read—little guesses about what will happen next, how a conflict will be resolved, which details will be important to the plot, which details will help fill in our sense of a character. Students should be encouraged to predict, to make sensible guesses as they read the novel.

As students work on their predictions, these discussion questions can be used to guide them: What are some of the ways to predict? What is the process of a sophisticated reader's thinking and predicting? What clues does an author give to help us make predictions? Why are some predictions more likely to be accurate than others?

Create a chart for recording predictions. This could either be an individual or class activity. As each subsequent chapter is discussed, students can review and correct their previous predictions about plot and characters as necessary.

Use the facts and ideas the author gives.

Use your own prior knowledge.

Apply any new information (i.e., from class discussion) that may cause you to change your mind.

Predictions

_____
_____
_____
_____

All rights reserved

Prediction Chart

What characters have we met so far?	What is the conflict in the story?	What are your predictions?	Why did you make these predictions?

All rights reserved

 © Novel Units, Inc.

Clue Log

Directions: When you read something you think might be important later on, write it down. See if you can solve the book's mystery.

Page	Clue (event or item)	Could have something to do with—

All rights reserved

Using Character Attribute Webs

Character attribute webs are simply a visual representation of a character from the novel. They provide a systematic way for students to organize and recap the information they have about a particular character. Attribute webs may be used after reading the novel to recapitulate information about a particular character, or completed gradually as information unfolds. They may be completed individually or as a group project.

One type of character attribute web uses these divisions:

- How a character acts and feels. (How does the character act? How do you think the character feels? How would you feel if this happened to you?)

- How a character looks. (Close your eyes and picture the character. Describe him/her.)

- Where a character lives. (Where and when does the character live?)

- How others feel about the character. (How does another specific character feel about the character?)

In group discussion about the characters described in student attribute webs, the teacher can ask for backup proof from the novel. Inferential thinking can be included in the discussion.

All rights reserved

Character Attribute Web

Directions: The attribute web below will help you gather clues the author provides about a character in the novel. Fill in the blanks with words and phrases that tell how the character acts and looks, as well as what the character says and feels.

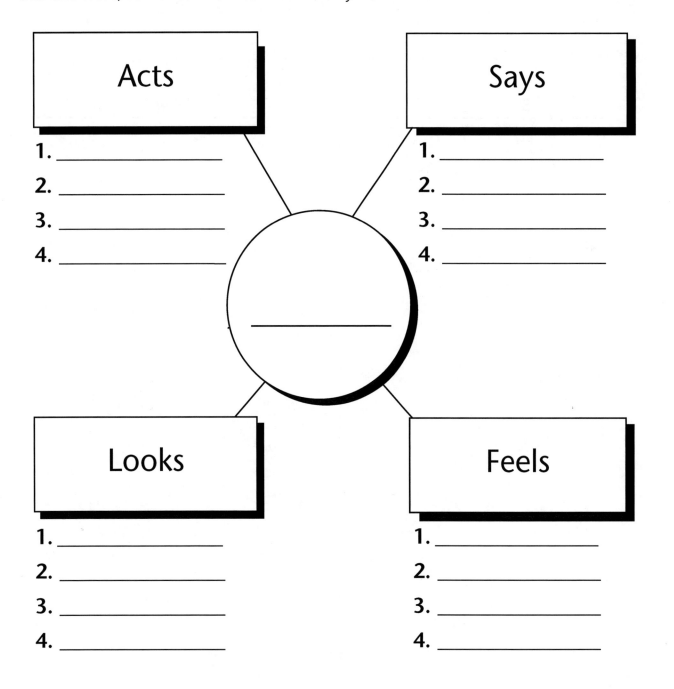

Acts
1. _____
2. _____
3. _____
4. _____

Says
1. _____
2. _____
3. _____
4. _____

Looks
1. _____
2. _____
3. _____
4. _____

Feels
1. _____
2. _____
3. _____
4. _____

All rights reserved

Character Analysis

Directions: On pages 98–122 of the novel, several characters start to change. Choose Wallace, Rachel, or Mr. Fogelman. List how the character was portrayed prior to this section in the Before column. List ways the character has changed in the After column.

Character Name_____

Before	After

All rights reserved

 © Novel Units, Inc.

The Daily News

Wednesday, October 2 • Section A, Page 1

_____

_____

_____

_____

_____

_____

_____

_____

_____

_____

_____

_____

_____

_____

_____

_____

_____

_____

All rights reserved

Character Chart

Directions: In the boxes across from each of the feelings, describe an incident or time in the book when each of the listed characters experienced that feeling. You may use "not applicable" if you cannot find an example.

	Wallace	Steve	Rachel	Mr. Fogelman
Frustration				
Anger				
Fear				
Humiliation				
Relief				
Triumph				

All rights reserved

 © Novel Units, Inc.

Pages 1–19

Wallace Wallace, the local football hero, is sent to detention during football practice for writing a novel review that his teacher, Mr. Fogelman, finds improper. Wallace is just being honest when he writes that he does not like the book *Old Shep, My Pal*. He serves detention during Mr. Fogelman's play practice, a play that just happens to be based on the book Wallace poorly reviewed.

Vocabulary
percolated (2)
slant (3)
toupee (3)
fluke (7)
titan (7)
mediocre (7)
grueling (8)
bamboozled (9)
earnestly (17)
intoned (19)

Discussion Questions

1. Why does Wallace feel it is necessary to always be truthful? (*because his dad lied so much that it caused his parents to divorce, pp. 2–3*)

2. Wallace states that "honesty wasn't just the best policy; it was the only one" (p. 2). How do you feel about this statement? (*Answers will vary.*)

3. Wallace never confronts his dad about his lies. Why isn't he honest with his dad about his feelings? (*Wallace feels that it is enough for his dad just to be his dad, not a CIA agent or an astronaut; however, he discovers that his dad will continue to lie and doesn't feel that confronting him will change anything. p. 3*)

4. Do you think Mr. Fogelman is justified in assigning Wallace detention for what he considers a poor review of a book? (*Answers will vary, but should be based on supporting evidence from the novel. pp. 4–5*)

5. Why is Wallace Wallace considered a football hero? Is this justified? Give reasons for your decision. (*Wallace sat on the bench most of his seventh-grade season, but was sent in as a blocker during the county championship game. He happened to be in the right place at the right time and fell on a fumbled football in the end zone in the final three seconds of the game to score the winning touchdown. Answers will vary on if the "hero" title is justified but should be supported by evidence from the novel. pp. 6–7*)

6. Why does Mr. Fogelman's detention time cause a problem for the football team? (*Wallace is assigned detention during football practice, and the players feel they need Wallace to practice for the opening game of the season. pp. 8–9*)

7. Why does Rachel call Trudi's comments "warning signs" (p. 13)? (*Rachel realizes that Trudi is more interested in boys than in acting and feels that her comments are a prelude to Trudi doing something silly and embarrassing. pp. 13–19*)

8. Do you think Wallace's second attempt at writing a review is an improvement over his first review? Defend your answer. (*Answers will vary. p. 16*)

9. Why do you think Rachel tells on Wallace for "writing a terrible review" (p. 17)? (*She is reading his review when Mr. Fogelman calls on her to read her lines, and she is not prepared. p. 17*)

10. How do you think Wallace reacts when Mr. Fogelman tells him he has a second day of detention? (*Answers will vary, but will probably include that he is upset because he still does not understand why his writing is unacceptable. p. 18*)

Supplementary Activities

1. Social Studies: Use print and Web resources to research where the phrase "the truth, the whole truth, and nothing but the truth" (p. 4) is commonly heard today. Discuss why it is used in this situation.

All rights reserved

2. Literary Analysis: The author uses the term "Rick-isms" (p. 9) to describe a play on words used by Rick Falconi. Keep a journal of "Rick-isms" used in the novel. Add others you hear to the list.

3. Writing: Write a letter to a favorite celebrity asking questions about his or her career, telling him or her about yourself, and asking advice on how to get started in the business.

4. Literary Devices: Working in pairs, locate at least two examples of each of the following types of literary devices in this section—simile, metaphor, and hyperbole. Examples: **Simile**—"Uncle Ted's toupee really *did* look like a small animal had crawled up onto his head and died there" (p. 3); **Metaphor**—"Rick looked daggers" (p. 6); **Hyperbole**—"I saw stars" (p. 5).

5. Story Map: Begin the Story Map on page 6 of this guide with information from the novel provided thus far.

Pages 20–45

Wallace discovers that his reassignment to detention prevents him from practicing football with the team even on weekends. School reporter Parker Schmidt misinterprets the situation and reports that Wallace is holding out for better grades. Wallace writes his third book review giving reasons why he hates the novel, but Mr. Fogelman doesn't accept it either. A mystery begins to develop as someone vandalizes the play set, and of course, all eyes turn to Wallace.

Vocabulary

mulling (21)
reverie (25)
mobbed (26)
uncanny (27)
chortled (28)
hyperventilating (41)
calisthenics (41)
ruckus (44)
snarl (45)

Discussion Questions

1. Why does Coach Wrigley tell Wallace that Mr. Fogelman is Wallace's problem? (*Since Mr. Fogelman has given Wallace detention until he writes an acceptable review, it is Wallace's job to write the review so he can get out of detention and return to football practice. p. 24*)

2. Do you think the Giants lost Saturday's game because Wallace did not play? (*Answers will vary, but should be supported with evidence from the novel. pp. 26–27*)

3. Why do you think Wallace describes Steve Cavanaugh as his ex-best friend? (*It could be that Wallace stole Steve's glory by scoring the touchdown at the championship game, or it could be something that happened earlier. Answers will vary. p. 27*)

4. Discuss the reasons why Parker's newspaper story about Wallace is incorrect. (*Students should provide examples of how Parker misinterprets the truth, doesn't have all the facts, exaggerates, doesn't tell the truth, etc. p. 31*)

5. If Wallace did not spray-paint the scenery board, why does he laugh when he sees it? (*He agrees with what it says and thinks it is funny. p. 33*)

6. Why doesn't Mr. Fogelman like Wallace's third review of the novel? (*The title labels the book as terrible, he claims Wallace's reasons aren't valid, and Wallace starts making suggestions to change the dialogue of the play. pp. 34–36*)

7. How does Rachel's latest letter to Julia Roberts show that her attitude toward Wallace is changing? (*Rachel states that Wallace is good-looking and that his ideas for changing the script are good. pp. 37–39*)

All rights reserved

 © Novel Units, Inc.

8. What do Trudi's answers to the quiz questions in *Teen Dazzle* magazine reveal about her character? (*not always totally honest, shallow minded, has a crush on Wallace, influenced by others' looks, defensive of Wallace, pp. 40–41*)

9. Why do the cast members like Wallace's suggestions for changing the play's dialogue? (*The play was written in 1951 and uses older expressions not used today. He suggests phrases that are commonly used by today's teens. p. 41*)

Supplementary Activities

1. Literary Analysis: Cavanaugh tells Wallace: "If you don't lie to anyone else in the world, you shouldn't lie to yourself either" (p. 28). This is an allusion to a famous quote: "This above all; to thine own self be true." Research the origin of this quote and write a paragraph telling how it compares with Cavanaugh's quote.

2. Writing: Write a newspaper story that *does* give the facts of why Wallace did not play in Saturday's game.

3. Prediction: Based on the evidence so far, use the Prediction Chart on pages 7–8 of this guide to predict who is vandalizing the play set and give reasons why he/she might be a suspect.

4. Art: Design a cover for *Teen Dazzle* magazine.

Pages 46–70

Wallace's friends try to help him get out of detention by writing reviews for him, except for Cavanaugh, who suggests that Wallace is behind the vandalism of the play set. Meanwhile Wallace continues to suggest script changes and tells the cast and director that the biggest problem is that the play does not have any action. He suggests reenacting onstage the motorcycle accident involving Old Shep. The cast is ecstatic, except for Rachel and Mr. Fogelman. The third act of vandalism occurs when a bucket of pepper drops onto the actors onstage, and Wallace rushes to the rescue. Mr. Fogelman decides to harness the energy of the students and allow the motorcycle scene.

Vocabulary
sabotage (50)
wheeze (51)
winced (52)
crimson (54)
queasy (55)
clammy (57)
berserk (58)
subdued (58)
reign (60)
pandemonium (60)
affable (60)
strident (60)
epidemic (67)

Discussion Questions

1. Why does Rick Falconi write a review for Wallace to give Mr. Fogelman? (*The Giants lose their second game of the season, and Rick is desperate to get Wallace back on the team at any cost, even if it means writing a review for Wallace to submit. p. 46*)

2. Why doesn't Wallace turn in Rick's review? What does this tell you about Wallace's character? (*He will not lie and say that someone else's work is his. It shows that he is honest and will not cheat. p. 47*)

3. Why is the team really losing their games? (*Last year the eighth graders made up most of the starters, and now they are in high school. p. 48*)

4. What does Wallace's mom mean when she says: "I'd have a better chance persuading a compass to point south" (p. 48)? (*It is almost impossible for a compass to point south, and it would be impossible to make Wallace be dishonest.*)

All rights reserved

5. Why does Wallace keep talking to Cavanaugh even though he is rude to him? (*Answers will vary.*)

6. How does Cavanaugh know that Wallace is not the guilty person? (*He was once Wallace's closest friend and knows him well enough to know he is always honest and tells the truth. p. 50*)

7. How do most of the play members feel about Wallace's guilt or innocence? (*Most think he is guilty but are willing to overlook it because of all the good advice he has provided. p. 52*)

8. When Trudi describes Wallace as "adorable, a football hero, and someone who could get us invited to all the coolest parties" (p. 54), what does it say about Trudi's character? (*Answers will vary, but could include that she is shallow and the stereotype of a typical teenage girl.*)

9. Why does Wallace feel there is a need to change Vito's script for the second time? (*He feels there is too much talking and not enough action. p. 56*)

10. When Wallace says that he "won't go anywhere near football practice" (p. 58), do you believe him? Why? (*Answers will vary, but probably will include yes, because he has been honest so far.*)

11. How do the students plan to solve the biggest problem of the play? (*Vito suggests using his mom's old moped, and Wallace suggests putting a toy dog on top of a remote-control car. Someone offstage will operate the remote, and the audience will see Old Shep run into the road. p. 59*)

12. What does this quote tell you about Mr. Fogelman's character: "This is our play, and this is how it's going to be performed. If anybody is unwilling to do that, let me know, and I'll begin looking for your replacement" (p. 61)? (*He is unwavering, obstinate, not open to suggestions, and close-minded.*)

13. What are some clues in Mr. Fogelman's memos that show that he is changing his attitude toward Wallace's suggestions? (*He agrees with Trudi: it's "a typical yawn of a school play..." [p. 64], describes rehearsals as nightmares [p. 64], and says "The frustration was mind-numbing" [p. 65].*)

14. Why does Mr. Fogelman call working off-Broadway "the good old days" (p. 65)? (*He feels that working and reasoning with kids is harder than working with non-professional actors who are in trouble with the law.*)

15. Why does Wallace laugh at the bucket of pepper prank? (*Answers will vary, but could include that he honestly thinks it is funny. p. 67*)

16. Why does Mr. Fogelman change his mind and allow the first scene to be staged according to Wallace's suggestion? (*He realizes what is missing from the play—a "happy, laughing, excited, united" [p. 68] cast. He decides to harness that energy and enthusiasm.*)

Supplementary Activities

1. Geography: Using clues from this section, find the general location of the setting of the novel on a map.

2. Point of View: Considering Mr. Fogelman's description of Nathaniel Spitzner on page 66, write the scene of the pepper prank from Nathaniel's point of view.

3. Drama: Act out the pepper prank incident to get a feel for the energy and enthusiasm of the students.

4. Writing: Mr. Fogelman writes memos to keep track of his day. Write several memos of things to do, then write your reaction to the event after it is done.

All rights reserved

5. Art: Draw the proposed first scene of the motorcycle accident as envisioned by Wallace.

6. Math: Take a survey of the class to see how many think Wallace is guilty. Show the results on a pie chart. Choose another character and take the survey again. Draw a line graph to show the results.

7. Literary Analysis: At the end of this section, Mr. Fogelman has an epiphany—a sudden realization of something really quite simple. Think of an epiphany you have had and write a paragraph about it.

Pages 71–97

The Giants lose their third game and blame Wallace for distracting them. Wallace, however, begins to discover clues to the identity of the person responsible for the vandalism, while Parker writes a story portraying Wallace as the principal's spy. Inadvertently, Wallace takes over the play with his suggestions—first to have Laszlo Tamas ride the moped, then to have Rory Piper as a Rollerblading dogcatcher, and finally to have the rock band Dead Mangoes perform!

Vocabulary
bellowed (73)
sourly (73)
skulking (76)
clambered (80)
snickered (80)
perplexed (82)
ominously (83)
retorted (85)
raved (86)
peevishly (87)
barged (88)
corridor (90)
ricocheted (91)
bickering (93)
cringe (94)

Discussion Questions

1. Do you think the Giants would have won if Wallace had been playing with the team? Give reasons for your answer. (*Answers will vary.*)

2. Do you think Wallace causes the Giants to lose their third game of the season? Give reasons for your answer. (*Answers will vary, but it is Wallace's presence at the game that distracts the players in the last seconds. However, good athletes should not be distracted by outside activities. p. 73*)

3. Do you think Coach Wrigley is sincere when he tells Wallace that losing the game is not Wallace's fault? Why? (*Coach Wrigley previously told Mr. Fogelman that Wallace being on the team would make no difference. pp. 63, 74*)

4. Why does Wallace like his principal, Mr. Chechik? (*Mr. Chechik is a bit like Wallace, as he is honest and gets straight to the point. p. 75*)

5. If Wallace believes that honesty is the best policy, why doesn't he tell the principal about the pepper in Feather's locker? (*Feather is his friend. Feather has a legitimate reason to have pepper in his locker. Wallace is not completely sure Feather is guilty. Wallace does not rat on his friends. p. 75*)

6. How do you know before you even read Parker's story that it will not be a fact-based story? (*Based on Parker's past stories and his actions, you expect to read a story full of Parker's opinions. pp. 76–78*)

7. Do you think Wallace is beginning to enjoy being at play practice? Give reasons for your position. (*Answers will vary.*)

8. Why does Rachel tell Mr. Fogelman about Wallace casting a Rollerblading dogcatcher in the play? (*She thinks Wallace is overstepping his bounds by casting parts in the play that do not exist in the book and by not talking to the director about it first. pp. 88–90*)

All rights reserved

9. Explain why Mr. Fogelman's memo: "A director must *never* lose control of his play" (p. 93) is an example of irony. (*When Mr. Fogelman makes the statement, he has already lost control of the play to Wallace and the other students. He is usually the last person to find out about any changes that are made.*)

10. **Prediction:** What is the "one course of action" (p. 97) that Mr. Fogelman plans to take? What can he possibly do that is so drastic? (*Answers will vary.*)

Supplementary Activities

1. Author's Style: The author uses a variety of techniques to write a humorous novel, such as figures of speech, sarcasm, funny incidents, silly names, etc. Find examples of these techniques that are humorous and make lists by categories.

2. Science: Use print and Web resources to find out about an Indian summer and why Wallace's clothes are inappropriate.

3. Foreshadowing: Using the Clue Log on page 9 of this guide, chart the clues and try to solve the mystery of who is vandalizing the play.

4. Drama: Facial expressions tell an audience how a person feels or what he or she thinks. Take turns showing different facial expressions and have the class guess the emotion.

5. History: Use print and Web resources to research Chinese water torture. Discuss whether Mr. Fogelman is accurate in his description on page 94 or if he is exaggerating.

Pages 98–122

Mr. Fogelman releases Wallace from his detention, but Wallace chooses to quit the football team and remain with the play. With a slip to Parker, Trudi starts the rumor that she is Wallace's girlfriend, which angers Rachel. Mr. Fogelman surprises everyone by joining the Dead Mangoes as their keyboard player for the play.

Vocabulary
plagued (98)
fixated (99)
flailing (99)
urgent (100)
mayhem (104)
propel (105)
savored (105)
stricken (106)
sneer (106)
auburn (109)
pathetic (110)
wheedle (110)
flustered (117)

Discussion Questions

1. What do you think causes Vito's swelling and why did he need to go to the doctor? (*He probably fell while learning to Rollerblade and injured himself enough to warrant a trip to the doctor. pp. 100–101*)

2. Discuss some clues that show Wallace is having a change of heart about working on the play. (*"In a weird way, I was even starting to feel I had a stake in it" [p. 101]. "What a great bunch of guys" [p. 103]! He plans to stop any football player from picking on the "drama nerds" [p. 103]. "I felt a surge of satisfaction as I stepped out into the hall" [p. 104]. "The Giants could take a lesson in classiness from the drama nerds…They'd earned my loyalty a whole lot more than the Giants had" [p. 106].*)

3. Why is Wallace suspicious when Mr. Fogelman praises Wallace's contributions to the play to the cast? (*Mr. Fogelman has been very upset over every suggestion Wallace has made to the cast so far, but now Mr. Fogelman is very calm, smiles at him, and praises him to the cast. pp. 101–102*)

All rights reserved

4. What is the real reason Mr. Fogelman dismisses Wallace's detention? (*Mr. Fogelman decides that if Wallace is gone, then the cast will have to listen to the real director's instructions, and he will have control of his play again. p. 102*)

5. Predict who might be responsible for the marble incident. Give reasons for your answers. (*Answers will vary.*)

6. Were you expecting Wallace to quit the football team and go back to work on the play? Why? (*Answers will vary.*)

7. Discuss who Wallace's real friends are and why. (*Answers will vary, but should include that most of the Giants won't even speak to him and that the drama club members always ask his advice and are supportive even when his detention has been lifted. pp. 102–108*)

8. How does Rachel react when she reads Parker's article? What does this reflect about how she feels about Wallace? (*She knows it is a lie and that Trudi told it to Parker. She is angry with Trudi, not Wallace. Answers will vary. pp. 113–114*)

9. Why does Wallace feel responsible for the slogan, *FEMME FATALE*, which is written on Trudi's locker? (*He has absolutely no interest in Trudi and totally ignores her and her advances, so he has no clue that she is responsible for Parker's remark in the article. He thinks Parker is out to get him. pp. 115–116*)

10. Why does Trudi state that the play is "the hottest ticket at school" (p. 117)? (*The football hero quit the team for drama, no one is allowed in rehearsals, rock music blares from the gym, eighth graders now talk to them, and everybody in school is interested in the play.*)

Supplementary Activities

1. Language: The middle-school students in the novel use a lot of contemporary slang words or phrases. Choose ten words or phrases and explain what the students really mean by them.

2. Author's Style: The author uses action verbs extensively throughout the novel to give life to the characters. Find five examples of action verbs. Choose one and draw a picture of the action.

3. Character Analysis: Use the Character Attribute Web on page 11 of this guide to analyze Trudi. After completing the chart, discuss whether or not you would want Trudi as your best friend and why.

4. Character Analysis: In this section, several characters start to change. Choose Wallace, Rachel, or Mr. Fogelman. Using the T-chart on page 12 of this guide, list how the character was portrayed prior to this section in the Before column. List ways the character has changed in the After column.

5. Foreshadowing: Continue adding clues to your Clue Log to solve the mystery of the vandal.

All rights reserved

Pages 123–150

When the drama club members come to Wallace's house to rake leaves without being invited, he discovers who his true friends are. However, after Wallace's football jersey is found amidst a pile of shredded scripts, even the drama club members jump to conclusions and blame Wallace for the attacks on the play. Mr. Fogelman forbids Wallace to come to the performance.

Vocabulary
mortified (124)
mystified (125)
sidled (125)
glowered (127)
bedlam (129)
cram (129)
cowering (132)
ushered (133)
mellow (134)
melancholy (141)
sulked (144)
bailed (144)
incensed (147)

Discussion Questions:

1. How would you interpret Wallace's dream? (*Answers will vary, but could include that he is torn between the two groups of friends. pp. 123–124*)

2. Why does Wallace misinterpret who his friends are when his mom calls him downstairs on Saturday? (*He has always called the football team members his friends, but has yet to realize that the drama club members are his friends, too. pp. 124–125*)

3. Discuss what Wallace means when he says, "I'd just made the switch to a different type of friend" (p. 126). (*Answers will vary.*)

4. Why does Cavanaugh come to Wallace's yard on Saturday? (*Answers will vary, but could reflect that he just wants to rub it in that the drama nerds are at Wallace's house. p. 128*)

5. Why is Wallace so angry when Cavanaugh calls him the "clown prince of the geeks" (p. 128)? (*Wallace is not angry that he calls him the clown prince, but that he calls his friends geeks. Wallace truly considers the drama club members his friends because they try so hard just for the sake of trying and not for glory. p. 128*)

6. Discuss what Coach Wrigley sees as the real problem of the Giants' football team. (*They blame others for their troubles instead of themselves. p. 131*)

7. Explain how Mr. Fogelman's section reflects a twist in stereotypes for rock band members and drama teachers. (*Mrs. Fogelman misinterprets the Dead Mangoes because of the way they look—long-haired boys wearing black jackets, driving an old van—but they are friends with the drama teacher. Mr. Fogelman lives in a clean suburban home, but likes to play with a rock band. pp. 132–133*)

8. Discuss what Mr. Fogelman means when he says, "But if you mold the play to showcase the talents of the students, the sky's the limit" (p. 134). (*Answers will vary, but could include that he realizes that the students are more important than the play.*)

9. Discuss the choice of words on the play flier on page 136. (*Answers will vary.*)

10. Do you think Trudi's marketing strategy, stating that the play is sold out to attract more attention, will work? Explain why or why not. (*Answers will vary.*)

11. Discuss the term "loosely based" in the play flier. (*Answers will vary.*)

12. What is Wallace's last suggestion for the play? Do you think they will use it? (*Wallace tells them not to let Shep die. Answers will vary. p. 142*)

13. When Rachel meets the football team on the field, how does she surprise them and break the stereotype of the drama nerd? (*She can run as fast as they can, and she catches the football. p. 147*)

All rights reserved

14. Cavanaugh makes a suggestion to Rachel about finding out the truth. He suggests she simply ask Wallace if he shredded the scripts. Discuss why this is such an obvious test of innocence or guilt for Wallace and why Cavanaugh is qualified to make the suggestion. (*Cavanaugh was Wallace's best friend and knows him better than anyone else. He knows that if Wallace says he didn't do it, that he is telling the truth. He also knows Wallace will not lie if he is guilty. pp. 149–150*)

Supplementary Activities

1. Writing/Art: Design a flier for the play. Include artwork. You may change the wording of the original flier.

2. Writing/Art: Design a playbill with artwork to be distributed to the audience the night of the play.

3. Debate: Either Wallace has been the culprit in the acts of vandalism, or he is being framed. Choose sides and debate the issue using clues from the novel to support your position.

4. Research: Wallace has a poster hanging in his room of a young George Washington chopping down a cherry tree. Use print and Web resources to research the history (or myth) behind this picture and discuss how it relates to Wallace.

5. Prediction: How do you think Mr. Chechik will react to the new version of *Old Shep, My Pal*? How do you think parents will react? Write a paragraph explaining your answers.

Pages 151–180

The cast and crew members decide to change the play's ending so that Old Shep lives. When Wallace discovers the football team members are attending the play, he decides to break the rules and attend the play to see if he can catch the culprit, who turns out to be Rachel's little brother Dylan. Wallace breaks tradition and lies by saying he is the guilty party so Rachel is not hurt over the truth about her brother.

Vocabulary
careening (160)
riling (161)
seethed (162)
riffled (164)
mesmerized (169)
plume (170)
mirth (172)
adulation (172)
enraptured (172)
detonated (175)
canine (176)
guffawed (179)

Discussion Questions

1. Do you agree or disagree with Rachel's statement, "…every time we did what he [Wallace] said, the play got better" (p. 153)? Support your answers with evidence from the novel. (*Answers will vary.*)

2. The novel does not tell Mr. Fogelman's reaction to the last-minute script change. What do you think it is and why? (*Answers will vary.*)

3. Why do you think the football team members go to the play performance? (*Answers will vary, but might include that they want to see what all the excitement is about.*)

4. How does the audience react to the performance? (*They love it; they give it a standing ovation; they dance along with the music, etc. pp. 158–159*)

All rights reserved

5. Why does Wallace compare hearing his dialogue onstage to making the winning touchdown? (*Both give him great pleasure and a sense of satisfaction, and the audience is excited over both. p. 159*)

6. Discuss whether or not you agree with Wallace when he says Cavanaugh belongs in drama. (*Answers will vary.*)

7. What do you learn about Rick when he says he plans to take pictures of the play for his friend Wallace? (*Rick is sincere and really is Wallace's friend. He does not get mad at Wallace for attacking him, but tries to help him find the real culprit. pp. 163–167*)

8. What is so ingenious about Dylan's final act to sabotage the play? (*It is Wallace's idea to let Old Shep live, so Dylan puts the cherry bomb on the toy dog. It looks like Wallace suggested it so that he can sabotage the play. p. 168*)

9. How does the audience react to such an unconventional ending to the play? Are they shocked and horrified? Why or why not? (*They roar with laughter and give a standing ovation for what they think is a great, hilarious ending. The rest of the play is so unconventional that this part just seems to follow in pattern and does not seem out of place. p. 171*)

10. Why does Wallace lie? (*Because Rachel had believed him, he lies to protect her from knowing that her own brother is the culprit. p. 173*)

11. Discuss the irony in the two pictures depicting Wallace jumping onto the exploding Old Shep and Wallace catching the winning touchdown last season. (*As Dylan says: "He's still got the moves!" p. 175*)

12. Discuss Julia Roberts' subtle suggestion that this story is a romantic comedy. (*Answers will vary, but the boy does get the girl...or vice versa! p. 177*)

13. Has Parker Schmidt's character changed at all? Why do you think so? (*No, because his stories are still filled with bias. pp. 175–176*)

14. Has Trudi Davis' character changed at all? Why do you think so? (*No, because she is still a silly, shallow-minded person. pp. 179–180*)

Supplementary Activities

1. Author's Style: The author uses suspense to build toward a climactic ending. List events that are suspenseful in the order they happen and discuss what makes them suspenseful.

2. Story Map: Complete your Story Map.

3. Writing/Music: Write lyrics for "Puppy Chow Blues" and "Shep's the Man (Even Though He's a Dog)." Perform the songs individually or as a group.

4. Art: Draw two pictures—one showing Wallace catching the winning touchdown and the other showing Wallace jumping onto the exploding toy dog. Make sure both depict Wallace in similar positions.

5. Writing: Using the graphic on page 13 of this guide, write a review of the play as a reporter from the local newspaper.

All rights reserved

Post-reading Discussion Questions

1. From whose viewpoint is the story told? How would the story be different if told from the viewpoint of another character, such as Dylan, Rick, or Steve? (*Each section is told from a different person's point of view as introduced by the title—Wallace, Rachel, Trudi, Parker, and Mr. Fogelman. Answers will vary.*)

2. Which character in the novel do you most relate to and why? (*Answers will vary.*)

3. What lessons did you learn from the novel and how can you apply them to your life? (*Answers will vary.*)

4. Discuss how you feel about Wallace's rule, honesty is the best policy, after reading the novel. Why do you feel this way? (*Answers will vary.*)

5. Do you agree or disagree that everyone has a talent, it's just a matter of finding it? Defend your answer. (*Answers will vary.*)

6. Discuss the qualities you think make a true friend. Are you that kind of person? (*Answers will vary.*)

7. Are Trudi and Nathaniel the types of friends you would like to have? Why or why not? (*Trudi is loyal, but she is silly and shallow. Nathaniel is dedicated to the play, but is whiny, obnoxious, and thinks only of himself.*)

8. Do you believe there is good in all people? Give reasons for your answer. (*Answers will vary.*)

9. Discuss the stereotypes presented by the characters in the novel. Give examples of how these characters break the stereotypes. (*Football players are seen as big and tough, but Wallace is actually good at directing a play. Drama club members are seen as geeks and nerds, but Rachel can run as well as any football player and catch, too. Teachers are seen as stuffy and uptight, but Mr. Fogelman joins a rock band, etc.*)

10. Would you like to have Mr. Fogelman as a teacher? Why or why not? (*Answers will vary.*)

11. Would you change the ending of the novel? If so, what would the new ending be? (*Answers will vary.*)

All rights reserved

Post-reading Extension Activities

1. Draw a comic strip of your favorite scene in the novel.

2. Write a haiku or an acrostic poem for each of three major characters in the novel that would describe each person.

3. Write a letter to the author asking what inspired him to write the novel.

4. Write the missing parts of the play staged in the novel and perform as a class.

5. Read one of the following books and compare and contrast with this novel: *Sounder* by William H. Armstrong, *Where the Red Fern Grows* by Wilson Rawls, or *Old Yeller* by Fred Gipson.

6. If Wallace were assigned to write a review of one of the above books, would it be a favorable review? Why or why not? Rewrite the ending of one of these books so that Wallace would approve of it.

7. Wallace makes the statement: "Go to the library and pick out a book with an award sticker and a dog on the cover. Trust me, that dog is going down" (p. 5). Test Wallace's theory by going to the library and conducting a search for books with pictures of dogs on the cover. Does the dog always die? Try to find a book where the dog lives.

8. Design a book jacket for the fictitious novel *Old Shep, My Pal* by Zack Paris.

9. Divide into small groups. Each group will be assigned a character from the novel. List the problems encountered by that character and then discuss alternative solutions to the problems.

10. Write a favorable review of *No More Dead Dogs* to entice someone else to read it.

11. Choose any story written by Parker Schmidt for the school newspaper. Write a list of interview questions that Parker should have asked. Partner with a classmate who now knows the facts and conduct the interview. Write a fact-based story of the event.

12. Construct a diorama of the stage setting for the play.

All rights reserved

 © Novel Units, Inc.

Assessment for *No More Dead Dogs*

Assessment is an ongoing process. The following ten items can be completed during the novel study. Once finished, the student and teacher will check the work. Points may be added to indicate the level of understanding.

Name _____ Date _____

Student   **Teacher**

_____   _____   1. Write ten original sentences using words from your vocabulary journal.

_____   _____   2. Choose a scene from the novel and rewrite it from another character's point of view.

_____   _____   3. Complete the Character Chart on page 14 of this guide with members of a small group.

_____   _____   4. Write a paragraph giving specific examples of various techniques used by the author to write a humorous novel.

_____   _____   5. Compare your completed Story Maps and Character Webs with members of a small group.

_____   _____   6. List three examples each of simile, metaphor, and hyperbole from the novel.

_____   _____   7. Role-play a scene from the novel.

_____   _____   8. Correct all quizzes and tests taken over the novel.

_____   _____   9. Keep a dialogue journal with one of the characters in the novel. Write questions you would like to ask the character about the character's feelings, reactions, beliefs, motives, or actions.

_____   _____   10. There are no pictures in the book. What picture or symbol would you use for each chapter?

All rights reserved

Linking Novel Units® Lessons to National and State Reading Assessments

During the past several years, an increasing number of students have faced some form of state-mandated competency testing in reading. Many states now administer state-developed assessments to measure the skills and knowledge emphasized in their particular reading curriculum. The discussion questions and post-reading questions in this Novel Units® Teacher Guide make excellent open-ended comprehension questions and may be used throughout the daily lessons as practice activities. The rubric below provides important information for evaluating responses to open-ended comprehension questions. Teachers may also use scoring rubrics provided for their own state's competency test.

Please note: The Novel Units® Student Packet contains optional open-ended questions in a format similar to many national and state reading assessments.

Scoring Rubric for Open-Ended Items

3-Exemplary	Thorough, complete ideas/information Clear organization throughout Logical reasoning/conclusions Thorough understanding of reading task Accurate, complete response
2-Sufficient	Many relevant ideas/pieces of information Clear organization throughout most of response Minor problems in logical reasoning/conclusions General understanding of reading task Generally accurate and complete response
1-Partially Sufficient	Minimally relevant ideas/information Obvious gaps in organization Obvious problems in logical reasoning/conclusions Minimal understanding of reading task Inaccuracies/incomplete response
0-Insufficient	Irrelevant ideas/information No coherent organization Major problems in logical reasoning/conclusions Little or no understanding of reading task Generally inaccurate/incomplete response

All rights reserved

 © Novel Units, Inc.